Discover & Learn

North & South America

This book is for pupils studying North and South America in KS2 Geography (ages 7-11).

It's jam-packed with facts, maps and questions covering locational knowledge of the Americas — perfect for exploring and understanding the whole topic.

Published by CGP

Consultant: Joanna Copley

Editors: Mary Falkner, Kelsey Hammond, Sharon Keeley-Holden, Sarah Pattison, Rosa Roberts, Rebecca Russell

Reviewer: Juliette Green

ISBN: 978 1 78294 981 7

With thanks to Alex Billings for the proofreading.

With thanks to Jan Greenway for the copyright research.

Printed by Elanders Ltd, Newcastle upon Tyne

Clipart from Corel®

Contents

North America

North America is one of the world's seven continents, and it has six main areas...

Fact Sheet: North America

Number of countries: 24 (some countries are small islands)
Area: About 25,000,000 square km (9,500,000 square miles)
Population (number of people): About 600 million
Largest country: Canada
Smallest country: Saint Kitts and Nevis (a Caribbean island)

St. Kitts and Nevis

Mountains, rivers and seas

This map shows North America's physical geography — its <u>mountain ranges</u>, <u>rivers</u> and <u>seas</u>.

Compare this map to the one on page 2. Which country is the Mackenzie river in? Which country is the Sierra Madre in?

Point to where the Mississippi river starts. Can you follow it with your finger to where it ends?

A continent of extremes...

North America has many different geographical features — canyons, waterfalls, desert plains, volcanoes, forests and glaciers. It also has some of the biggest cities in the world.

South America

South America is also one of the seven continents in the world. You can see the countries and territories that make up South America on the map below.

The Amazon Rainforest covers 40% of South America. It is very biodiverse — there are around 2.5 million different species of plants and animals living there.

La Paz (the capital city of Bolivia) is the highest capital in the world. The city is 3,600 metres up in the clouds.

Every year, the world's biggest carnival is held in the streets of Rio de Janeiro. It lasts for five days and around 5 million people take part.

South Georgia is famous for its enormous penguin colonies. About 7 million penguins live on the island including King Penguins.

On the tip of South America are many small islands called Tierra del Fuego. They are shared between Chile and Argentina. The most southerly point is Cape Horn.

Fact Sheet: South America

Number of countries: 15
Area: About 18,000,000 square km (7,000,000 square miles)
Population (number of people): About 440 million
Largest country: Brazil
Smallest country: South Georgia and the South Sandwich Islands

Rio de Janeiro, Brazil

The amazing Amazon

There are lots of rivers in South America, but the most famous is the mighty Amazon. This map of the physical geography of South America shows just how long it is.

The Amazon basin is a huge area of land in South America covered by rainforest. All the water in the basin will eventually drain into the Amazon River.

The Amazon River is over 6,400 km (4,000 miles) long — this makes it the second longest river in the world.

One of the most important places in the world...

More than 10% of all animal species in the world live in the Amazon rainforest. Most of these are insects, such as butterflies, ants, and arachnids (like spiders and scorpions).

Natural Americas

There are ten different types of biome spread across the Americas.
A biome is an area with certain plants and animals that have <u>adapted</u> to the climate there.

Tundra
Climate: Cold and dry all year.
Plants: Small plants that are able to survive the cold, like moss.
Animals: Arctic hares, polar bears, seals.

Alpine
Climate: Cold, windy and snowy all year.
Plants: Tough bushes, which can withstand the climate.
Animals: Animals with thick fur like alpacas and mountain goats.

Temperate Grassland
Climate: Warm summers and cold winters.
Plants: Grasses.
Animals: Bison, foxes, armadillos.

Tropical Rainforest
Climate: Hot and wet all year.
Plants: Thousands of tree and smaller plant species.
Animals: Jaguars, giant otters, frogs, tarantulas.

Deciduous Forest
Climate: Warm summers and cold winters.
Plants: Trees that lose their leaves in winter like oak.
Animals: Raccoons, owls, rabbits, bobcats.

Which type of biome would you most want to live in?.

Which of the animals on this page have you heard of before? Are there any you haven't heard of?

☐ Polar Desert

Climate: Cold and dry all year.
Plants and Animals: These places are too cold for plants or animals to live.

■ Coniferous Forest

Climate: Temperate (cool summers and cold winters) or polar (cold and dry all year).
Plants: Evergreen trees like spruce and pine.
Animals: Brown bears, owls, squirrels, deer.

■ Savannah

Climate: Hot all year. Wet for half of the year and dry for the other half.
Plants: Grasses with few trees.
Animals: Rhea, capybara.

■ Mediterranean

Climate: Hot, dry summers and mild winters.
Plants: Some forests (coniferous and deciduous) and lots of shrubs.
Animals: Wolves, badgers.

☐ Desert

Climate: Hot and dry.
Plants: Small tough plants like cacti that don't need lots of water.
Animals: Lizards, desert fox, coyote.

Every biome is unique...

Some have big predators like bears and jaguars, some have dangerous amphibians like poison dart frogs, and some have beautiful birds like parrots and eagles.

Moving to the Americas

The Americas are full of people from many different cultural backgrounds
(originally from different countries with different traditions and languages).
Certain periods in history have affected how society has developed over the years.

In ancient times

The indigenous people of the Americas were divided into many tribes, such as the Inuit
in Canada, the Quechua in South America, and the Powhatan in what is now the USA.

The Powhatan Tribe

The Powhatan tribe lived a <u>simple lifestyle</u>. They lived in
small round houses called <u>wigwams</u>, or in larger <u>longhouses</u>.
They <u>hunted</u> and grew <u>crops</u>, such as beans and squash.
They also <u>fished</u> using canoes made from hollowed-out tree trunks.

Some very developed civilisations also formed, such as the Aztec and the Inca...

The Inca

The Inca empire stretched all the way from <u>Ecuador</u> to <u>Chile</u>.
The Inca were <u>clever engineers</u>. They worked out smart
ways of building cities and watering their crops.
The most famous city is <u>Machu Picchu</u> in Peru.
Parts of it are <u>still standing</u> because it was built so <u>well</u>.

European invasion

In 1492, Christopher Columbus became the first European to sail to the <u>Caribbean</u>.
He <u>claimed</u> the land for Spain. Soon after, Spain and Portugal set up colonies
all over <u>Central</u> and <u>South America</u>.

In the 1600s, Britain, France, and the Netherlands successfully set up <u>colonies</u>.
Eventually, much of the Americas was under <u>control</u> of European governments.

Many Europeans <u>migrated</u> (moved) to the Americas and <u>took land</u> from the indigenous people,
leading to <u>wars</u>. They also brought new <u>diseases</u> with them to the Americas, which they
passed on to the tribes. Millions of indigenous people were <u>killed</u> by the fighting and disease.

Forced to the Americas

Starting in 1503, millions of <u>Africans</u> were brought to the Americas to work as slaves for European settlers. Mostly they worked on <u>sugar plantations</u> and were treated <u>very badly</u>. Many slaves had <u>children</u> in the Americas and their children became slaves too.

Slavery was gradually <u>abolished</u> (made illegal) in the 1800s.
To replace the slaves, the plantation owners took workers from <u>India</u> and <u>China</u>.
These workers were also poorly treated.

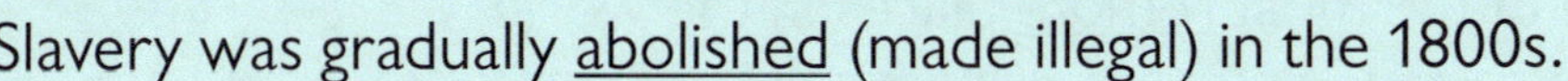

Historical influence

Right up until the <u>present day</u>, people from all around the world have continued to move to the Americas, often in search of a better life. Almost everyone in the Americas today has <u>ancestors</u> from another part of the world. There are over <u>300 languages</u> spoken there, and people of every <u>religion</u>.

The <u>history</u> of the Americas helps us understand its culture <u>today</u>...

Into the melting pot...

The USA is often called a 'melting pot' — different cultures have melted together into American culture. Some things we think of as American were brought from elsewhere. For example, hamburger meat and the word kindergarten were introduced by Germans.

Greenland & Alaska

Both <u>Greenland</u> and <u>Alaska</u> are partly in the <u>Arctic</u>. The Arctic is the area north of the <u>Arctic Circle</u> — an imaginary line that goes all the way around the world (see page 34). Greenland and Alaska contain some of the most <u>remote</u> places in the world, far away from towns and cities. Many places are also very <u>difficult</u> to get to.

The Arctic is sometimes called <u>the Land of the Midnight Sun</u>. In northern Greenland the Sun <u>doesn't set</u> for almost four months in the summer.

Even though Greenland is part of the North American <u>continent</u>, it's actually a region of the <u>Kingdom of Denmark</u>.

<u>Denali</u> in Alaska is the <u>tallest mountain</u> in the whole of North America.

The most important industry in Greenland is <u>fishing</u>. In Alaska, the <u>oil and gas</u> industry is most important.

Greenland is almost completely covered by an <u>ice sheet</u> and glaciers, so most people live around the <u>coasts</u>. One third of the population live in the capital city, <u>Nuuk</u>.

Alaska <u>isn't</u> a country. It's one of the 50 <u>states</u> of the USA. <u>Juneau</u>, the capital city, is only accessible by <u>boat</u> or <u>plane</u> because it's surrounded by steep mountains.

A life on the ice

The indigenous people of Arctic Alaska and Greenland are called the Inuit. Almost everyone living in Greenland is Inuit. Inuit culture in Greenland has changed a lot, especially in the last fifty years, but many of their traditions have remained.

The traditional way of life

Inuit people needed to be good hunters in order to survive. They hunted seals, walruses and reindeer for food and used the skins and bones to make clothes, tents and boats. In summer they gathered berries and roots to eat too.

They were nomads (travellers), never staying in one place for long. Sleds pulled by dogs were used to travel across the ice and small paddle boats called kayaks were used to travel, as well as hunt and fish on the water.

There are still some Inuit who live this way today.

A changed culture

These days, most Inuit people have jobs in shops or offices so they can buy food and pay for modern comforts like electricity. Some Inuit still hunt for all their food, but now they often use rifles and travel by snowmobile. Animal skins are warmer than modern fabrics, so some Inuit still make clothes from them.

Hunting is becoming more difficult. To protect wildlife, limits have been set on the number of animals that can be hunted. Also, warmer temperatures mean that the ice is becoming thinner. The Inuit are adapting to these changes, by hunting different animals and fishing from boats instead of from sea ice.

Do you think it's fair to limit the number of animals the Inuit can hunt? Why or why not?

Disappearing traditions?

Inuit culture is changing for many reasons — modern jobs, imported goods, changing temperatures and hunting limits. Only time will tell if their ancient traditions will continue.

Northern and Western Canada

Canada is the <u>second largest</u> country in the world, and has a huge variety of landscapes including mountains, rivers, lakes, and prairies. It's divided into thirteen sections called <u>provinces</u> and <u>territories</u>. Here are seven of them...

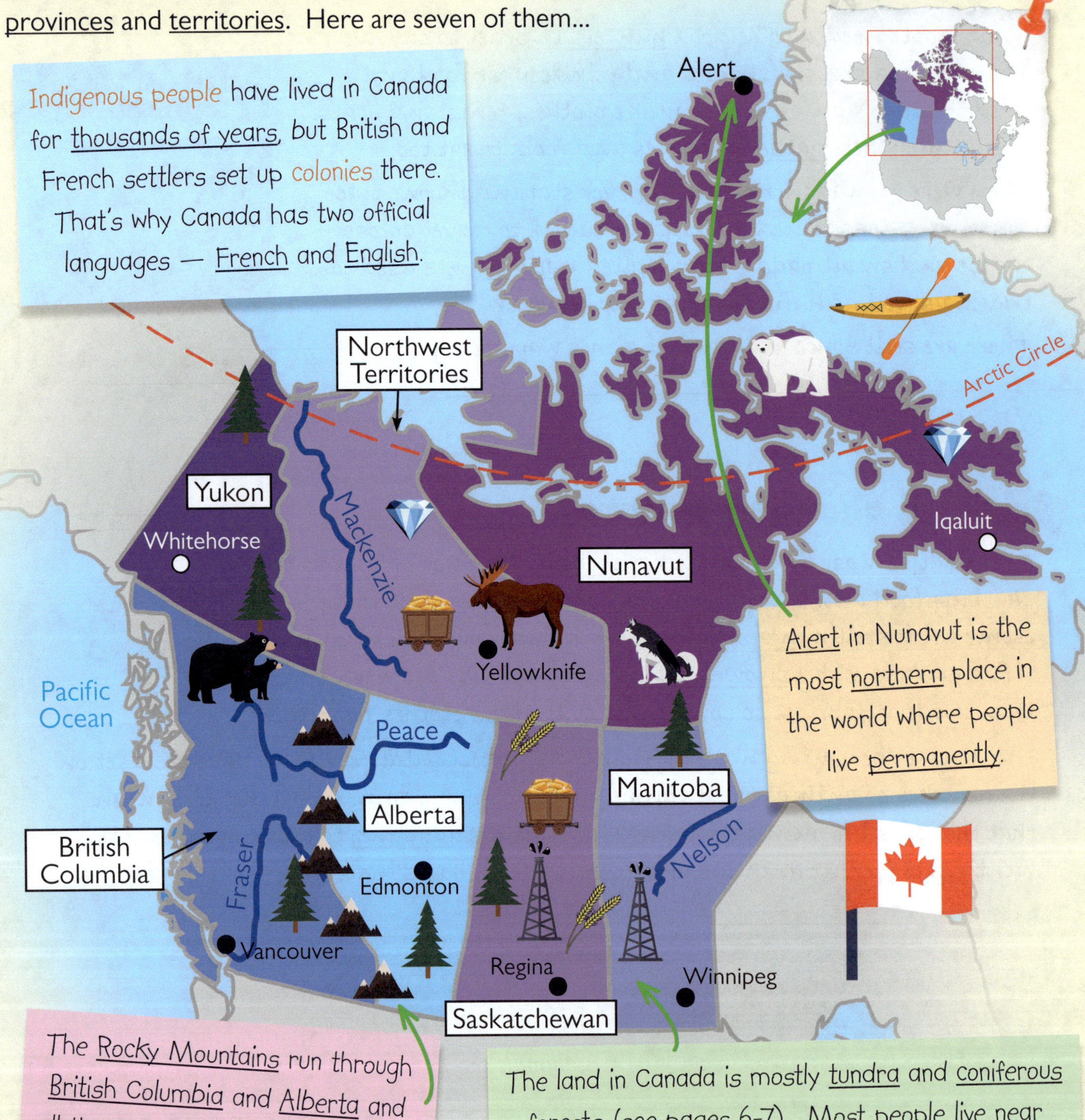

Like chalk and cheese

Canada is so <u>big</u> that different regions can seem like different worlds. Even within a single province or territory the landscape and climate can <u>vary a lot</u>. Nunavut in the <u>north</u> and <u>Saskatchewan</u> on the <u>southern</u> border have very different industries, landscapes and climates.

REGION 1

Nunavut

A lot of Nunavut is <u>tundra</u> — the ground is rocky and in some places it stays <u>frozen all year</u>. Nunavut has a <u>polar climate</u> and is <u>cold all year</u> — in some places it can be -36 °C in the winter, and only 6 °C in summer.

<u>Mining</u> is a big industry here — gold, copper and diamond are all mined in the area. Nunavut's population is mostly <u>Inuit</u>, so traditional <u>arts and crafts</u> are also part of the economy.

Nunavut is Canada's <u>largest</u> territory, but very few people live there. The places where people do live are scattered very <u>far apart</u> from each other.

REGION 2

Saskatchewan

Saskatchewan is known as a <u>prairie</u> province. However, it is not all prairie. The northern half is covered in <u>coniferous forest</u>.

Saskatchewan summers are <u>sunny and warm</u> (about 25 °C) but the winters are <u>extremely cold</u> (often below −20 °C).

Agriculture, mining and <u>oil production</u> are major industries in Saskatchewan. <u>Crops</u> such as canola (which is used to make oil) and wheat are grown on huge farms on the <u>flat</u> prairies. The main mined products here are <u>potash</u> (for fertiliser), and <u>uranium</u> (for nuclear fuel).

The high life...

Different landscapes and climates in Canada make a big difference to how people live. For example, many houses in Nunavut are built on stilts. This stops the heat from the houses melting the frozen ground. If the ground defrosted, the houses would sink.

Eastern Canada

The East of Canada is where most of the <u>big cities</u> are.
It's also where the famous <u>Great Lakes</u> are found, as well as <u>Niagara Falls</u>.

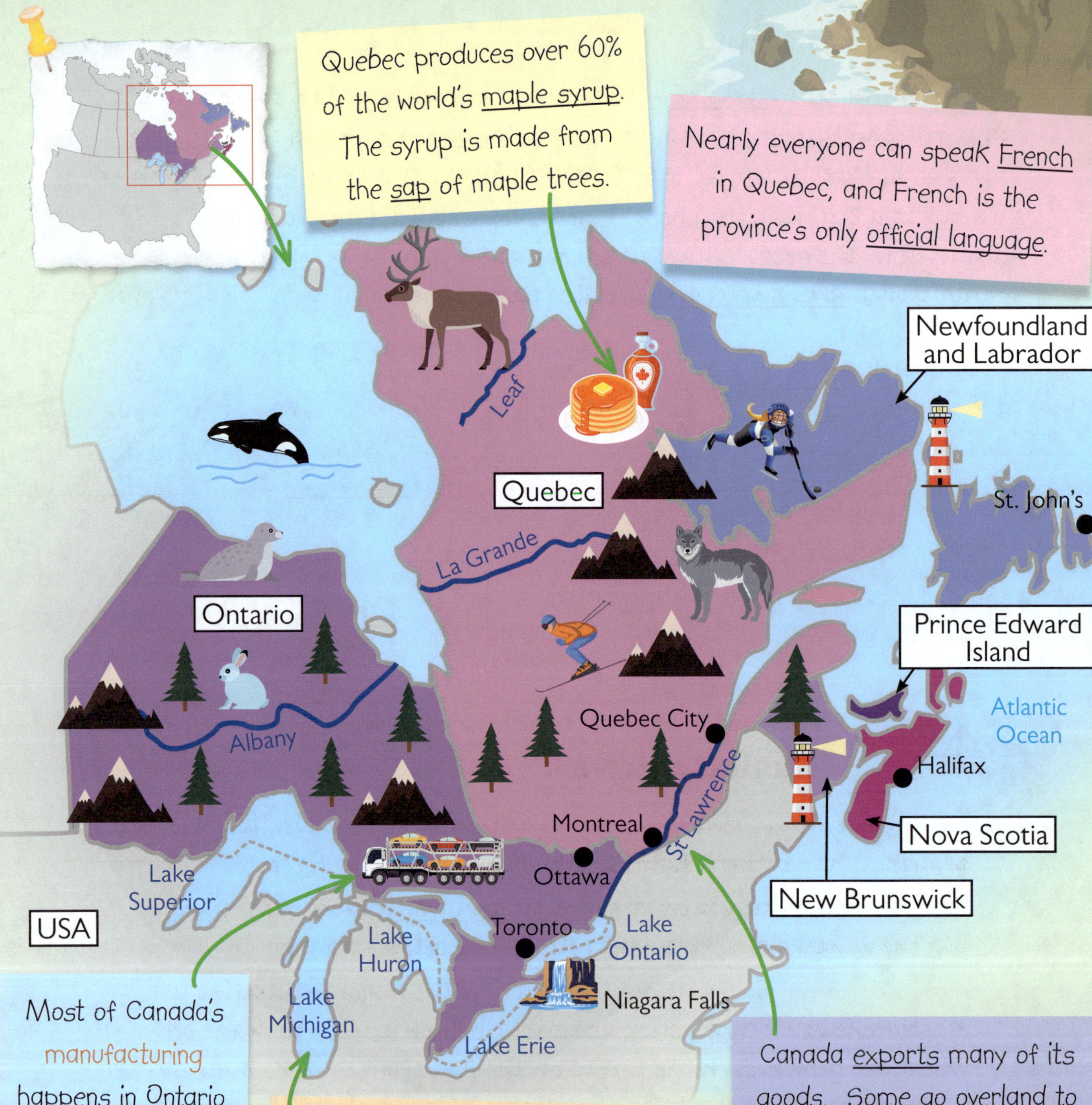

A hard-working waterfall

Niagara Falls is a group of <u>three waterfalls</u> on the border between Canada and the USA. It is part of the <u>Niagara River</u>, which carries water from Lake Erie to Lake Ontario. Niagara Falls isn't just impressive to look at — it also supports two different <u>industries</u> in the area, the <u>hydroelectric</u> industry and the <u>tourism</u> industry.

INDUSTRY 1 — Hydroelectricity

There are several hydroelectric power plants around the Falls. They use the <u>energy</u> of the <u>falling water</u> to generate enough electricity to power <u>millions of homes</u>.

<u>Over half</u> the water in the Niagara River doesn't actually reach the Falls. Instead, it's diverted through underground <u>tunnels</u> to power plants, where it turns <u>turbines</u> to <u>generate electricity</u>. The water is then returned to the river further <u>downstream</u> below the Falls.

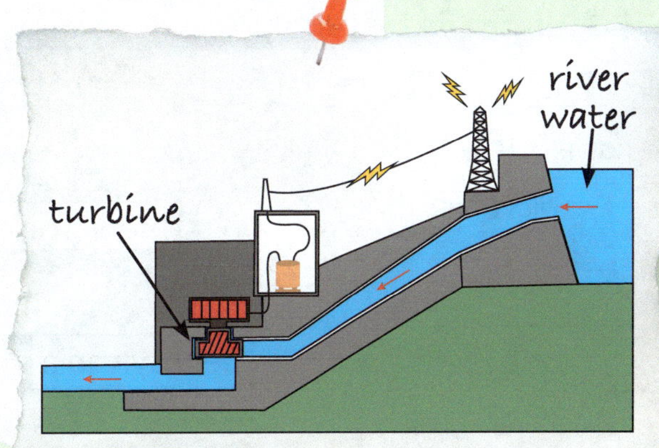

INDUSTRY 2 — Tourism

Niagara Falls is one of the <u>most popular</u> tourist attractions in the world. There are about <u>13 million</u> visitors each year. Tourists spend a huge amount of <u>money</u> around Niagara Falls. A lot of what they spend is in hotels and restaurants. This creates thousands of <u>jobs</u> in the area.

To make sure that the Falls looks <u>spectacular</u> for tourists, the power companies aren't allowed to divert <u>too much</u> water away from the Falls. More can be diverted at <u>night</u> and in <u>winter</u> when there are fewer visitors.

Wandering waterfalls...

Niagara Falls is slowly moving upstream due to erosion of the rocks by the powerful water. Over the last twelve thousand years they've moved an amazing seven miles.

USA – East Coast

The United States of America (USA) is split into 50 states. They all have their own capital cities, flags and people to represent them in government.

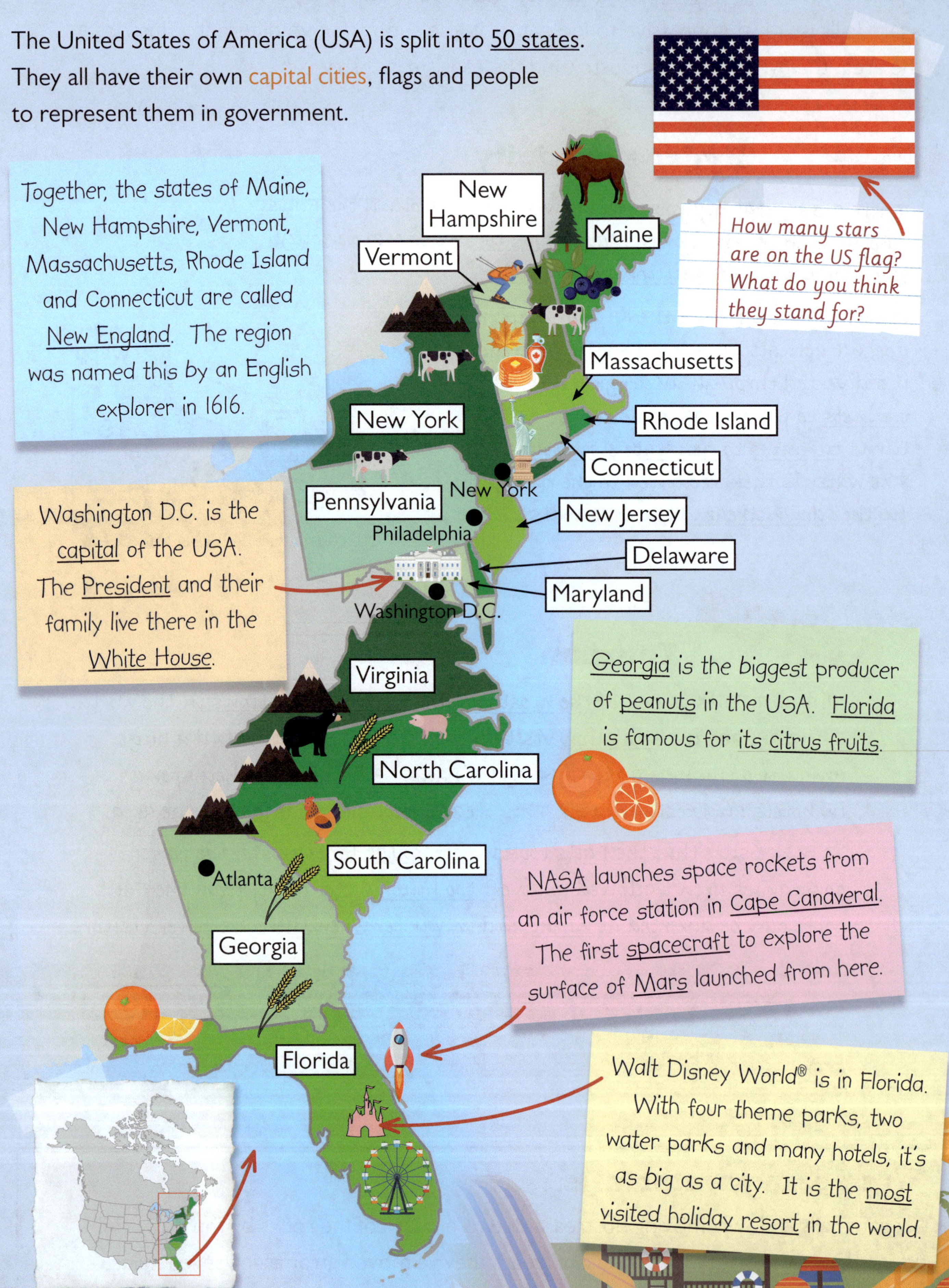

Together, the states of Maine, New Hampshire, Vermont, Massachusetts, Rhode Island and Connecticut are called New England. The region was named this by an English explorer in 1616.

How many stars are on the US flag? What do you think they stand for?

Washington D.C. is the capital of the USA. The President and their family live there in the White House.

Georgia is the biggest producer of peanuts in the USA. Florida is famous for its citrus fruits.

NASA launches space rockets from an air force station in Cape Canaveral. The first spacecraft to explore the surface of Mars launched from here.

Walt Disney World® is in Florida. With four theme parks, two water parks and many hotels, it's as big as a city. It is the most visited holiday resort in the world.

Sun, sand and snow

The East Coast stretches for over <u>1500 miles</u> from north to south.
This is a huge distance so it's not surprising that the northern
states have a very different climate from those in the south.
Here are two places, one in the north and one in the south,
which attract tourists for very different reasons.

DESTINATION 1

Vermont

Vermont <u>summers</u> are <u>warm</u>, with an average temperature of about 18 °C.
People come to Vermont in summer to <u>hike</u> or <u>bike</u>, or just enjoy the <u>scenery</u>.

In <u>autumn</u> (or 'fall' as it's called in America)
the leaves on Vermont's many <u>maple trees</u> turn
such amazing colours that many visitors come
to see them. This is known as <u>leaf peeping</u>.

Vermont has very <u>cold winters</u>, with an average
temperature of about -6 °C. It's even colder in the
mountains and they get lots of <u>snow</u>, which makes them perfect for <u>skiing</u>.

DESTINATION 2

Southern Florida

Southern Florida has a <u>tropical</u> climate. The <u>summers</u> are <u>hot</u> (about 28 °C),
<u>humid</u> and <u>rainy</u>. The <u>winters</u> are short and <u>warm</u> (20 °C on average).

The weather makes it perfect for beach holidays and
<u>water sports</u> like <u>parasailing</u> and <u>surfing</u> all year round.

The downside of Florida's <u>location</u> is that it is often hit by
damaging <u>hurricanes</u> (storms with very strong winds),
which form over the <u>Atlantic Ocean</u>.

Stars and stripes...

The first thirteen states that formed the United States of America were all British colonies
on the East Coast. The thirteen stripes on the US flag represent these first states.

USA – In the Middle

After taking control of land in the east, European settlers began to move _west_ and create new colonies. These middle states are famous for _farming_, especially of _wheat_ and _cattle_. They also produce most of the USA's _oil_.

Curious crops

Like the eastern states, there is a variety in the types of crops grown in this region. The climate and the land affect what crops can be grown where. Here are two examples of different states and the crops they grow.

CROP 1

Wheat in Kansas

In Kansas, the main crop grown is wheat. This is partly because the land is flat with rich, fertile soil (soil that's full of nutrients that help plants to grow).

There are lots of different types of wheat. In Kansas, winter wheat is grown as this is best suited to the climate. This is planted in the autumn but it doesn't start to grow until the weather gets warmer in the spring. Then it's harvested in late June, before the temperature and humidity get too high.

Almost every state in the USA grows wheat, but some of the states in the centre of the country grow so much that they've been nicknamed 'America's Breadbasket'. The crops grown here are very important for feeding the whole country.

Compare this map to the one on page 18. Which states are not part of the 'breadbasket'?

CROP 2

Rice in Louisiana

Rice is one of the main crops grown in Louisiana. It needs lots of water to grow properly, so the floodplains of the Mississippi River are perfect. They are flat, muddy and frequently covered with water from the regular heavy rain or flooding rivers. The weather also suits rice growing — wet, warm summers and mild winters.

Mega farming...

Kansas doesn't just grow wheat, it mills a lot of it into flour. In fact, it's the top flour-producing state. Every year they produce enough flour to make 36 billion loaves of bread.

USA – Out West

The western part of the USA has lots of different types of landscape, including <u>forest</u>, <u>desert</u>, <u>mountain</u> and prairie. It's a region full of contrasts — from <u>hi-tech companies</u> and <u>film studios</u> to vast <u>wildernesses</u> where mountain lions roam.

<u>Mount St. Helens</u> is a <u>volcano</u> in Washington. It <u>erupted</u> in 1980 and sent a cloud of ash nearly 20 km into the air. People over <u>260 km</u> away heard the explosion.

The south-western states have large <u>deserts</u>. The <u>hottest</u> air temperature <u>ever recorded</u> on Earth was measured in <u>Death Valley</u>, California. It reached a scorching 57 °C.

'<u>Silicon Valley</u>' is a famous area near <u>San Francisco</u>. Lots of big technology companies are based here, like <u>Facebook</u>®, <u>Apple</u>® and <u>Google</u>™.

Earthquakes are very common in California. That's because it's near a tectonic plate <u>boundary</u> (a place where two of the Earth's tectonic plates <u>meet</u>). This is called the <u>San Andreas Fault</u> and it runs all the way up California.

Natural wonders

Some of the most amazing natural places in the world are in the western USA, including the Grand Canyon and Yellowstone National Park.

FEATURE 1

The Grand Canyon

The Grand Canyon is an enormous, steep-sided valley in Arizona. It was carved out by the Colorado River, which wore down the rock over 6 million years. This is called erosion.

The canyon is almost 2 km deep and nearly 450 km long — that's almost as long as the entire island of Ireland. At its narrowest point the canyon is over 6 km across, and at its widest point it's an amazing 29 km across.

The sides of the canyon look stripy because they're made up of different layers of rock formed over millions of years.

FEATURE 2

Yellowstone National Park

Yellowstone National Park in Wyoming sits on top of an active volcano. This creates impressive geysers. A geyser is a vent in the Earth's surface. Hot water and steam shoot from them every so often. This happens because magma close to the surface heats underground water until it boils. The pressure builds up and causes the geyser to erupt suddenly.

The most famous geyser in the park is called Old Faithful because it erupts about once every 90 minutes.

The West really is wild...

As well as its amazing rock features, the West is also home to some incredible animals like grizzly bears, bison, wolves and North America's biggest bird — the California condor.

Mexico and Central America

Central America is a group of countries in the southern part of the North America continent. The official language in most of these countries is Spanish, which is a result of the Spanish colonisation of Central America in the 1500s.

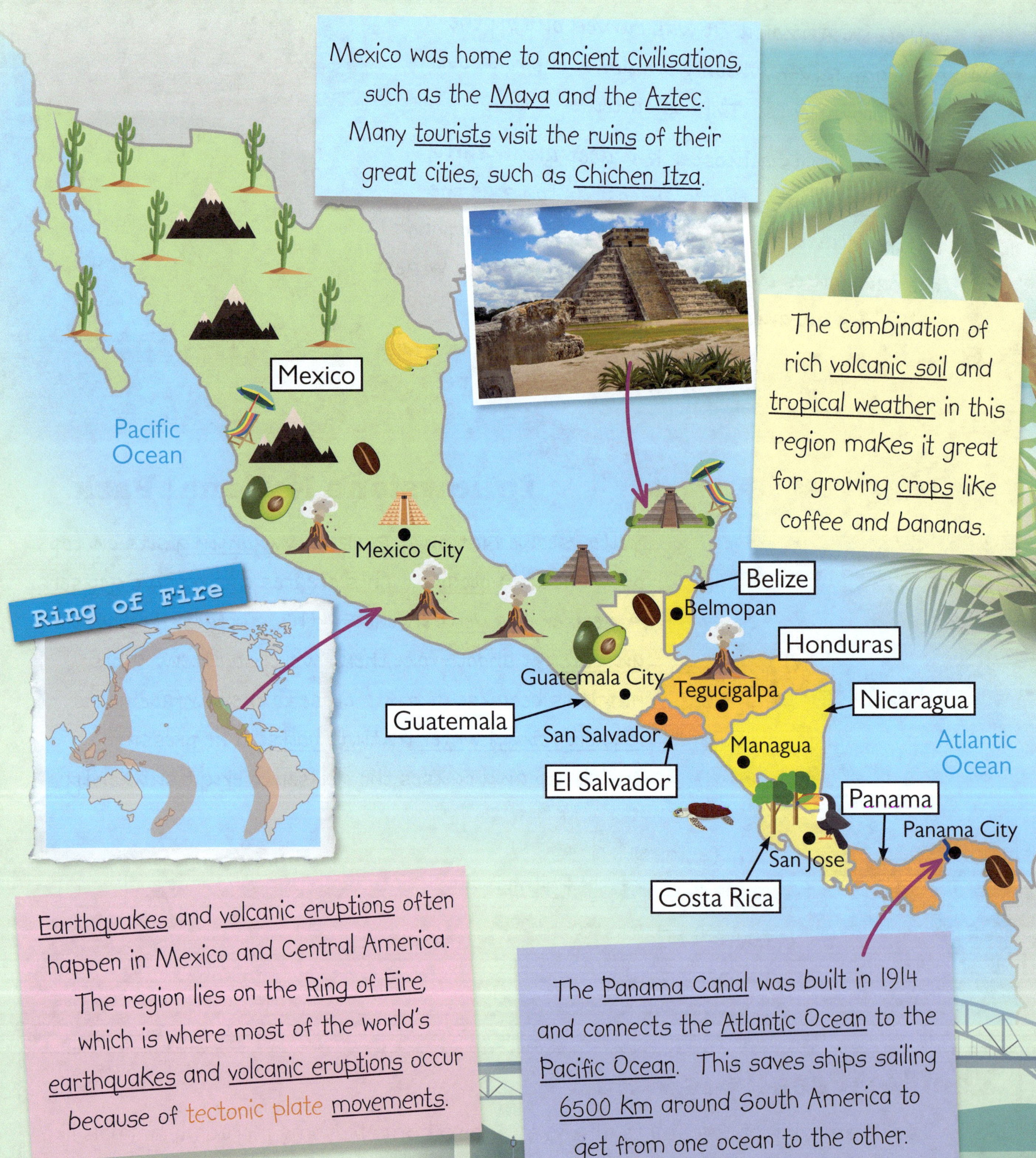

Land of contrasts

Mexico has a wide range of <u>temperatures</u>, which has resulted in some very different biomes.
This has made it one of the most biodiverse countries in the world.
Unfortunately, <u>human activity</u> is affecting Mexico's biomes.

Chihuahuan Desert

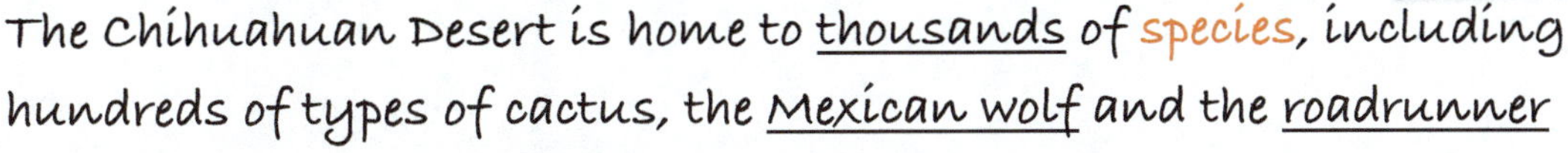

Part of the Chihuahuan Desert lies in <u>northern Mexico</u>.
This desert has hot summers and cold winters.

The Chihuahuan Desert is home to <u>thousands</u> of species, including
hundreds of types of cactus, the <u>Mexican wolf</u> and the <u>roadrunner</u>
— a bird that can run up to 20 miles per hour.

However, the land is being <u>changed</u> by <u>farming</u>. Farm
animals eat all the grass, leaving nothing but <u>shrubs</u>.
Some wild animals, such as the <u>Mexican pronghorn</u>,
have almost completely <u>disappeared</u> from the desert
because so much of their habitat has been lost to farming.

Lacandon Jungle

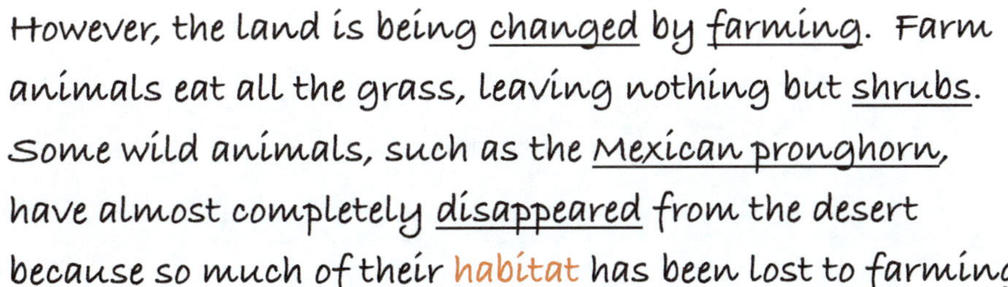

The tropical <u>rainforests</u> of Mexico are <u>warm</u> and
<u>wet</u> all year. The <u>Lacandon Jungle</u> is an area of
rainforest that contains many endangered animals,
like <u>jaguars</u>, <u>spider monkeys</u> and <u>scarlet macaws</u>.

Much of the rainforest has been destroyed by <u>slash-and-burn
agriculture</u>. This is when farmers <u>burn down</u> parts of the
rainforest to make room for <u>crops</u>. The <u>ash</u> from the fires
makes the soil <u>fertile</u>, but only for a couple of years.
Then the farmers have to burn down <u>more</u> of the
rainforest and more animals lose their habitats.

Balancing act...

Farmers in this region are often poor and need to use the land to earn money and
grow food, but sometimes this has terrible effects on the natural environment.
Governments often try to work with farmers to make sure the land is protected.

The Caribbean

The Caribbean Islands are located to the <u>east</u> of Central America.
They make up a huge archipelago in the Caribbean Sea.

The <u>Dominican Republic</u> is home to the biggest <u>gold mine</u> in the Americas. As well as gold, they export a lot of sugar, coffee and silver.

<u>Bananas</u> are grown on many of the Caribbean islands. Most of them are <u>exported</u> by ship to countries such as the <u>UK</u>.

Can you think of any other foods we eat in the UK that come from other countries?

The Bahamas

Havana

Cuba

Haiti

Atlantic Ocean

British Virgin Islands

Puerto Rico
San Juan

US Virgin Islands

Anguilla

Cayman Islands

Jamaica

Dominican Republic

St. Kitts and Nevis

Antigua

Montserrat

Guadeloupe

Dominica

Haiti is one of the world's <u>poorest</u> countries. Many people <u>don't</u> have access to clean drinking water. <u>Hurricanes</u> and <u>earthquakes</u> have caused huge problems for the country. Because it's so poor, the buildings are <u>not well-built</u>, and are easily destroyed.

Caribbean Sea

Martinique

St. Lucia

St. Vincent

Aruba

Curaçao

Grenada

Barbados

Port of Spain

Grenada is known as the <u>Spice Isle</u>. It's an important producer of <u>nutmeg</u> and <u>cocoa</u>.

Trinidad and Tobago

A horrible history

The <u>history</u> of the Caribbean is very important for understanding what it's like today. The actions of European colonists in the 1500s completely <u>transformed</u> the <u>culture</u> and <u>land use</u> on the islands.

THEN

Plantations and slavery

European colonists made the indigenous people of the Caribbean work for them on huge farms called <u>plantations</u>. They grew valuable crops like <u>sugar</u> and <u>tobacco</u> to sell back to Europe. Many indigenous people <u>died</u> because of <u>diseases</u> brought over by the settlers.

A <u>huge number</u> of workers were needed on the plantations, so millions of people were kidnapped from Africa and forced to work as <u>slaves</u>.

The slaves knew they'd <u>never</u> get back to Africa, but they did their best to keep their <u>culture</u> alive, for example, through traditional music, dancing and stories.

<u>Calypso music</u> grew from African music brought over by slaves. Slaves weren't allowed to talk to each other so they communicated through Calypso music instead.

NOW

A combination of cultures

<u>Over half</u> the Caribbean population are <u>descended</u> from African <u>slaves</u>. This means African culture influenced Caribbean <u>food</u>, <u>music</u> and <u>religion</u>. The influence of <u>European settlers</u> can also be seen in Caribbean culture.

<u>Salsa</u> music and dancing originated in <u>Cuba</u> and has both <u>African</u> and <u>Spanish</u> influences.

<u>Cricket</u> was introduced to the Caribbean by British colonists. It's <u>very popular</u> in the Caribbean, and a big part of the <u>culture</u>.

A land of many languages...

Haitian Creole and Papiamento are two of the official languages in the Caribbean. They're mixtures of European and African languages. Spanish, English, French and Dutch are also official languages because of the European colonists who settled there.

Andean Nations

The countries on the west coast of South America share the <u>Andes</u> mountain range.
From north to south it's an enormous <u>7200 km</u> (4500 miles) long.

Life in the clouds or life in the city?

People's lives high in the Peruvian Andes are very different to those who live in urban (built-up) areas like Lima. The climate and terrain (landscape) are big influences on how people live and make money.

The Peruvian Andes

The land in the Andes is rocky and steep and the weather can be cold and dry. Despite the tough landscape, around 9 million people live in the Andes in Peru. Many of these people are farmers. They grow crops like potatoes and corn wherever they can — even on the sides of the mountains. They use llamas to transport goods across the rough land. Many people in the Andes live simple lives and can grow or make most of the things that they need.

Lima

Down in the city, the weather is warmer. It's easier to get around as people can use cars and bicycles on the flatter land. There are shops to buy food and clothes, and jobs in manufacturing, banking and other businesses.

Not everyone can get a well-paid job though, and there are big differences between the rich and the poor in Lima. There are slums (very poor and over-crowded areas) in the city, with high levels of crime and disease.

Mixing cultures in the city...

In the mountains in Peru, many people are descended from the Incas and have quite a traditional culture. In contrast, in Lima, all the people moving to the city from other places bring their own cultures which creates a mixture of traditions.

Brazil and the Guianas

The <u>Amazon rainforest</u> covers a lot of the north-east side of South America. The countries in this area are all trying to <u>balance</u> industries like <u>logging</u> and mining with protecting the forest.

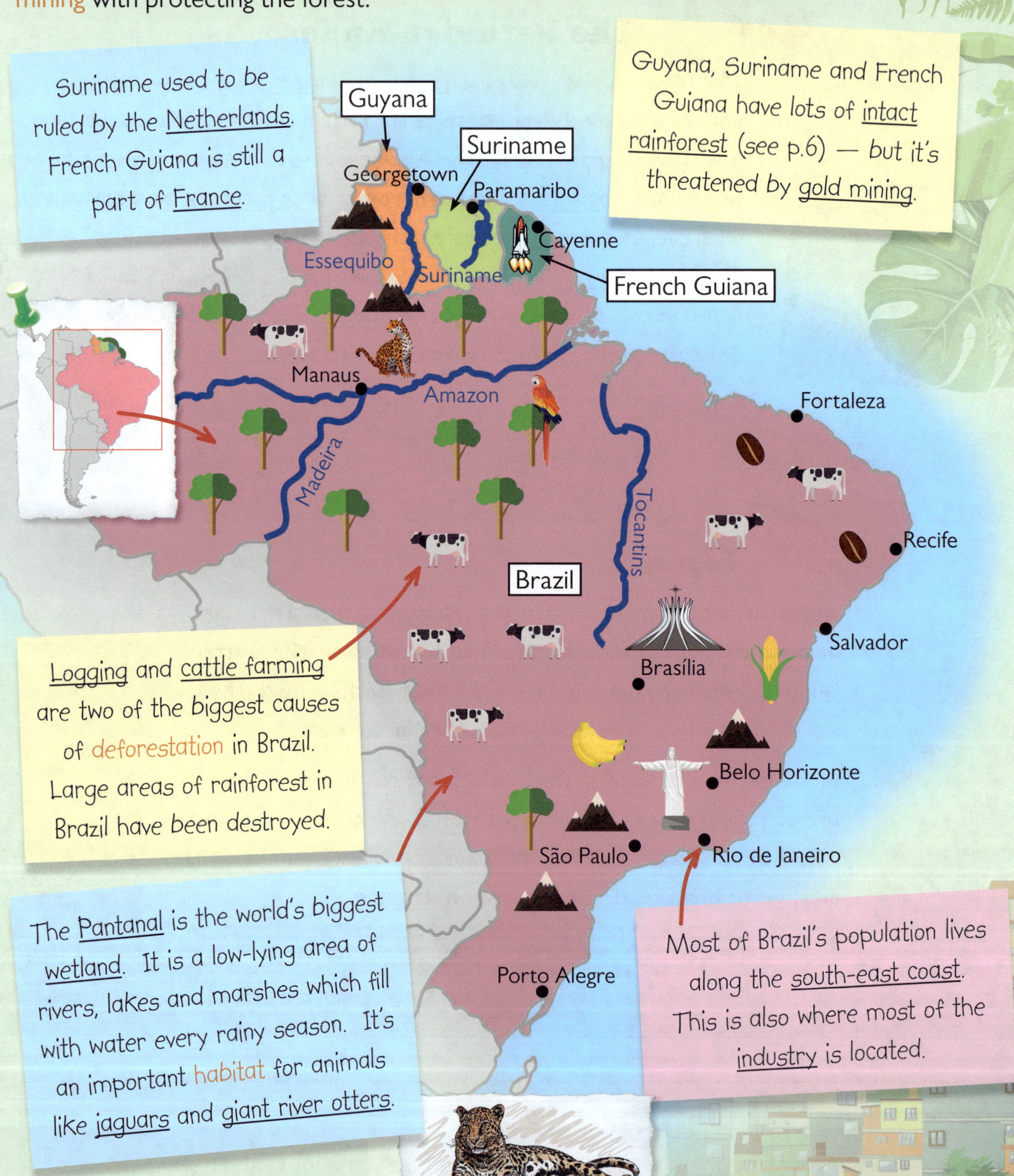

Tribes in trouble

Tribes have lived in the forests of South America for thousands of years, but growing numbers of farms and mines are threatening their ways of life. Some tribes are holding on, but there are groups of people that have already been forced to leave their land for good...

The Yanomami

The Yanomami are a tribe of around 38,000 people. They live in a large area stretching across northern Brazil and southern Venezuela. The Yanomami live in large round houses called yanos with up to 400 people inside. The men hunt for animals, and the women grow crops and harvest honey. Illegal mining is the main threat to the tribe, as miners cut down the forest they rely on. People coming from outside the area have also brought in diseases which have harmed the Yanomami people.

The Guarani

Around 50,000 Guarani people live in Brazil. Over the last few decades, the Guarani have lost a lot of their traditional lands to cattle farming. With less land it can be difficult for them to grow enough food. Some groups of Guarani people have lost all of their land — many of the people that this has happened to end up living in tents by the roadside. Some people have to leave their communities for long periods of time to work on sugar plantations in poor conditions for very little money.

Home sweet home...

Brazil has laws to protect the rights of the tribes that live there, including their right to live on their traditional lands. But it can be difficult to make sure that everyone follows these laws. And when people don't follow them, it can make life very difficult for the tribes.

The Southern Cone

The <u>Southern Cone</u> is another name for the countries at the very bottom of South America. They have the <u>Andes</u> mountains to the west, plus enormous plains, deserts and cities.

The <u>Atacama</u> desert is a huge, flat area of land at the base of the <u>Andes</u> mountains. It's quite <u>cool</u> even in summer. It's also the <u>driest</u> desert in the world.

The <u>Pampas</u> is a big <u>plain</u> that covers a large area of Southern Argentina. South American cowboys called '<u>gauchos</u>' have kept cows on the plains since the 1800s. Some crops like corn and wheat are grown here too.

The west coast of Chile lies on a tectonic plate boundary (where two plates meet). Lots of <u>earthquakes</u> and volcanic <u>eruptions</u> happen in this area. The most powerful earthquake ever recorded occurred in Chile in 1960.

<u>Ushuaia</u> is the most southerly city in the world. It's part of Argentina and is on the island of <u>Tierra del Fuego</u>. The city has over 70,000 residents and is the closest port to the Antarctic.

Life in the city

Buenos Aires is the capital city of Argentina, and is the biggest city in the Southern Cone. Its large economy attracts lots of people to move there looking for better lives. But there are big <u>divides</u> between the city's rich and poor.

THE NORTH

The Rich

The <u>north</u> of the city is the home of some of the richest residents. They own businesses, or work in the busy <u>financial</u> sector of the city, and make <u>lots</u> of money. The rich live in modern <u>apartment blocks</u> or <u>mansions</u> which have gates and guards around them to separate them from the rest of the city. Children from rich families often attend <u>private schools</u> and <u>university</u>, so they can also get well-paid jobs.

THE SOUTH

The Poor

Some of the poorest people in Buenos Aires live in the <u>south</u> of the city. Some of them are <u>migrants</u> who moved there from rural areas. Many can't find work, or have <u>low-paid</u> jobs in factories. They often don't make enough money for food, clothes or good quality housing. They live in <u>slums</u> called 'villas miserias', which have badly built houses that are cramped and falling apart. Children can't afford to go to private school or university. <u>Crime</u> can be a big problem.

Not enough money to live on...

In 2002, poverty in Argentina hit a record high, with 9 million people living on less than £1.50 a day. The number has fallen since then, but many Argentinians are still very poor.

The Southern Islands

In the <u>South Atlantic Ocean</u> lie the Falkland Islands and South Georgia and the South Sandwich Islands. They are <u>British territories</u>, but the UK and Argentina <u>disagree</u> over who should govern them. The islands are <u>cold</u> and difficult to get to, so not many people live there.

The Falkland Islands

This region is home to thousands of <u>penguins</u>. They're perfectly <u>adapted</u> for the cold. They have a thick layer of <u>blubber</u> (fat) under their skin to keep warm.

South Georgia

There's a <u>research base</u> run by British <u>scientists</u> on South Georgia. People come here to study the <u>environment</u> and the <u>wildlife</u>.

The <u>Drake Passage</u> is an 800 km stretch of water between Antarctica and South America. It's one of the most <u>dangerous</u> areas to sail through in the world.

South Sandwich Islands

Would you like to explore any of these islands? Why or why not?

The South Sandwich Islands are about <u>1500 km</u> from Antarctica. They are actually a line of big <u>volcanoes</u> created at a tectonic plate boundary (where two plates meet). Some of them are still <u>active</u> today.

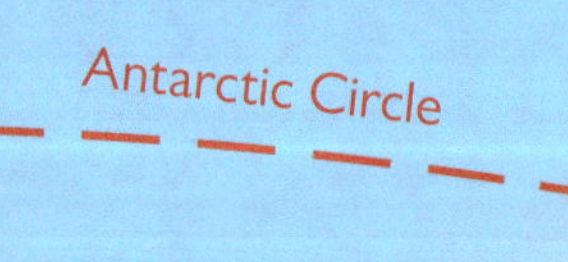

Towns at the end of the Earth

The extreme environments on these islands make them <u>difficult</u> places to live. Some have no <u>settlements</u> on them at all, with only colonies of <u>penguins</u> and other animals living there.

The Falkland Islands

The Falkland Islands are a group of islands covering about 12 000 square kilometres (4700 square miles). The weather is very <u>windy</u> and <u>cool</u> all year. The average temperature in winter is 2 °C and in summer it's only 8 °C. The islands are <u>rocky</u> and <u>steep</u> with cliffs at the coast. Around 3000 people live <u>permanently</u> on the islands. Over half of those live in the <u>capital</u>, Stanley. Fishing is the largest economic activity, with other industries including <u>tourism</u> and farming <u>sheep</u> for <u>wool</u>.

South Georgia and the South Sandwich Islands

On these islands, temperatures are <u>cold</u> all year round, with lots of snow. The strong winds create <u>blizzards</u>. The average summer temperature is just 4 °C. In winter it's -1.5 °C and the days are short, with very little daylight.

In the past, some seal and whale hunters lived on the islands, but there are no permanent residents now. People do visit the islands though. <u>Scientists</u> come there to do research and <u>tourists</u> come to see the <u>wildlife</u>, like orcas and penguins.

Stormy weather...

Life can be really tough when you're living as close to the South Pole as the people on these islands are. If you live there, you do get to see some amazing wildlife though.

World Zones

The continents of North and South America stretch from the north to the south of the globe. Each region's climate is linked to where on the globe it is located.

Circles on the Earth

There are five important imaginary lines around the Earth. They split the planet up into zones:

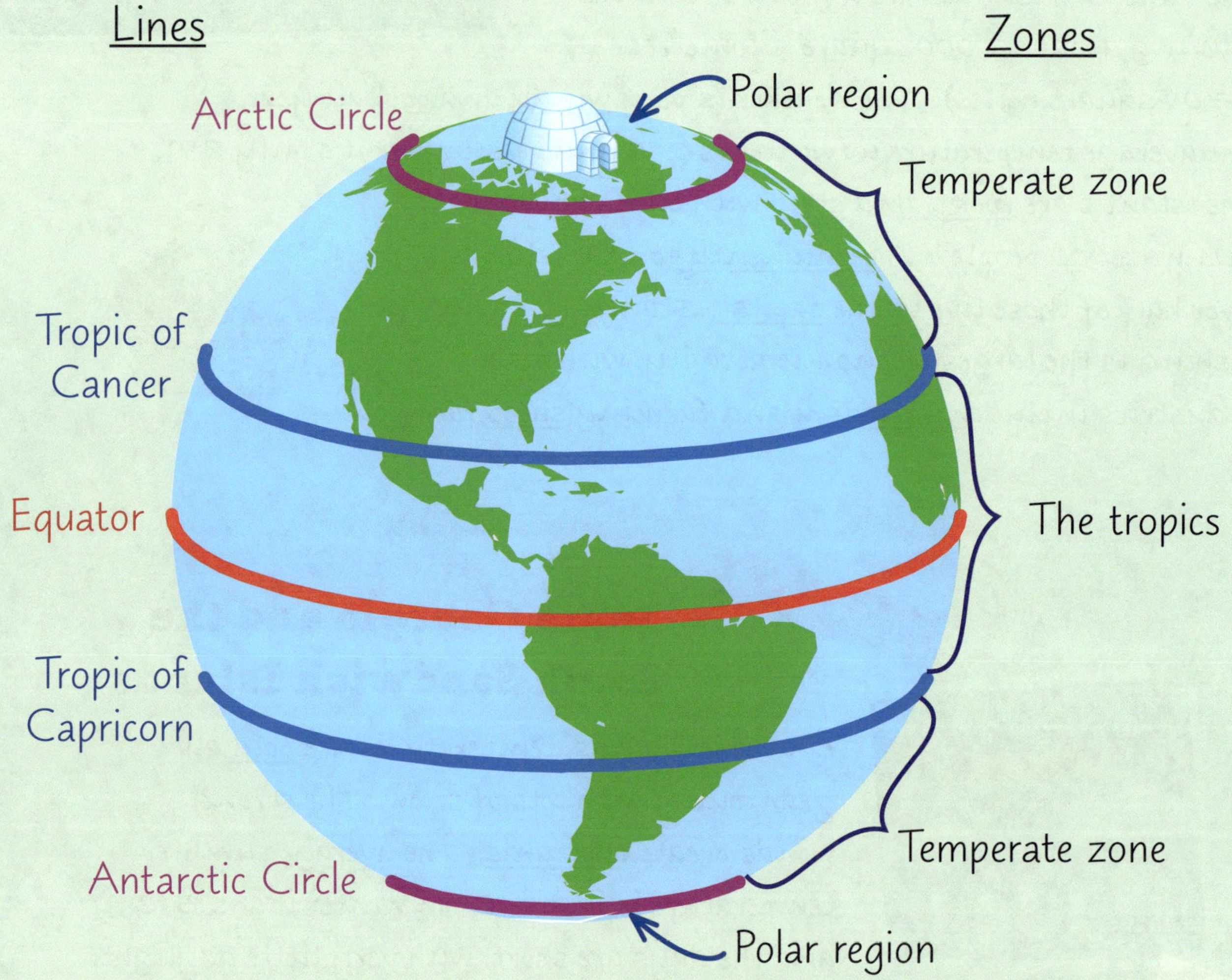

Lines
Zones
Arctic Circle
Polar region
Temperate zone
Tropic of Cancer
Equator
The tropics
Tropic of Capricorn
Temperate zone
Antarctic Circle
Polar region

Each point on Earth has a latitude measured in degrees (°).
This tells you how far north (N) or south (S) of the Equator the point is.
Some examples are shown on the right.

Alert: 83° N
Montreal: 46° N
Equator
0°
La Paz: 16° S
Cape Horn: 56° S

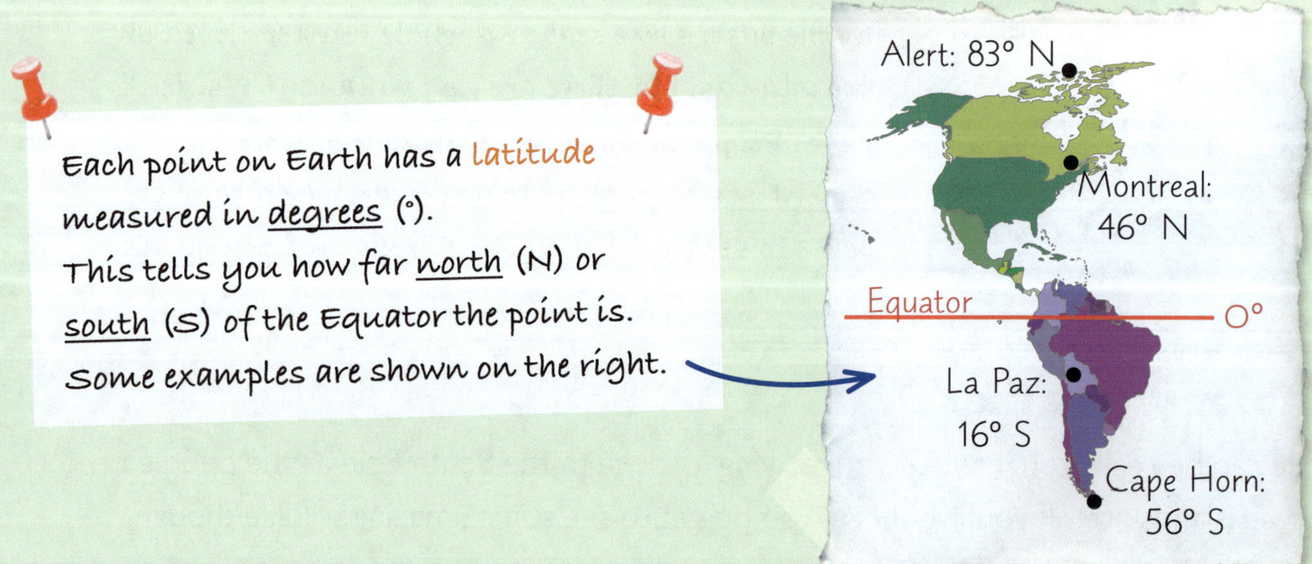

North of the Arctic Circle is a polar region. North America lies across the Arctic Circle, so it is partly in a polar region. There's another polar region south of the Antarctic Circle, but South America doesn't cross this line.

The polar regions are really cold and are covered with ice caps.

The area between the Tropic of Cancer and the Tropic of Capricorn is known as the 'tropics'. Almost everywhere in this region is always hot. Different climates and biomes are found here, such as desert, tropical rainforest and tropical grassland.

The areas between the tropics and the polar regions have a temperate climate, which has cold winters and dry summers. The temperate zones have four seasons — spring, summer, autumn and winter.

Places in the temperate zones tend to be warmer the closer to the tropics they are. The parts of the temperate zones closest to the tropics are called the subtropics.

Which of these three zones do you think the UK is in?

The subtropics are hot enough to grow fruits such as oranges and avocado.

It isn't all about latitude...

Temperature doesn't just depend on how far north or south you are. It's also affected by altitude, nearby ocean currents, and whether you're in the centre of a large land mass.

Glossary

agriculture	Another word for farming.
altitude	The height of a place in relation to sea level.
archipelago	A group of islands.
biodiverse	Having a big variety of plant and animal species.
biome	An area which has similar plants, animals and climate.
canyon	A deep, steep-sided valley that usually has a river at the bottom.
capital city	A city where the government of a country or state is based.
civilisation	A society in a particular area.
climate	What the weather is usually like and has been like for years.
colony	A group of settlers living together in one place.
colonisation	Taking over an area or country that already has other people living in it.
colonist	A person who settles in a new area or country.
continent	A large mass of land and the islands closest to it. The Earth has seven continents.
deforestation	Cutting or burning down large areas of trees.
economy	The system of how a country or region makes and manages its money.
endangered	A plant or animal that is at risk of becoming extinct (disappearing forever).
erosion	When rock is broken down into small bits or worn away by water or the wind.
export	To send goods to another country to sell.
extinct (species)	Species of plants and animals which have completely died out.

floodplain	The land around a <u>river</u> which normally becomes <u>flooded</u> when the river rises.
glacier	A huge mass of <u>ice</u> that moves across the land <u>very slowly</u>.
government	A group of people that make the <u>laws</u> in a country.
habitat	The place where an animal or a plant normally <u>lives</u>.
indigenous (people)	The <u>original</u> inhabitants of a place, and their descendants who still live there.
industry	An economic activity that involves collecting <u>raw materials</u> (like <u>coal</u>) or making <u>products</u> in <u>factories</u>.
latitude	How far <u>north</u> or <u>south</u> a place is from the <u>equator</u>.
magma	<u>Hot liquid rock</u> under the Earth's surface.
manufacturing	Industry that involves making <u>products</u> in <u>factories</u>.
mining	<u>Digging</u> up different types of <u>rock</u> and <u>mineral</u> from the ground.
port	A place where ships can <u>load and unload</u> people and goods.
prairie	A large area of <u>land</u> covered with <u>grass</u>.
renewable (energy)	Energy that comes from a <u>source</u> that <u>won't run out</u>, like <u>wind</u>, the <u>Sun</u> or moving <u>water</u>.
rural (area)	An area that doesn't have lots of <u>buildings</u>, like the <u>countryside</u>.
slave	Someone who is <u>owned</u> by another person and <u>forced to work</u> for <u>no money</u>.
species	A group of <u>plants</u> or <u>animals</u> that are similar and can <u>reproduce</u> with each other.
tectonic plate	<u>Pieces</u> of the <u>Earth's crust</u> that <u>float</u> on the <u>mantle</u>.
urban (area)	An area that is a <u>town</u> or <u>city</u>.

Acknowledgements

Cover photo: © iStock.com/BardoczPeter.

Some paragraphs in this book are based on real-life events. However, some situations, characters and dialogue have been changed or invented for dramatic purposes – any similarity to a person, living or deceased, in these areas is merely coincidence.

Graphics used through this book: (push pin) © blackred/E+/via Getty Images. (lined paper) © Subjug/iStock / Getty Images Plus. (torn paper) © tomograf/iStock / Getty Images Plus.

Section One — The Continents
p2 (map icons) © drmakkoy/DigitalVision Vectors/via Getty Images. p4 (map icons) © drmakkoy/DigitalVision Vectors/via Getty Images.
p4 (Argentinian street) La Inspiratriz / Alamy Stock Vector. p6 (llama) © drmakkoy/DigitalVision Vectors/via Getty Images.
p8 (ship) Image on page 8 used under licence from Shutterstock.com. p9 (slaves on sugar plantation) © English School/Look and Learn.

Section Two — Northern America
p12 (oil well) Image on page 12 used under licence from Shutterstock.com. p16 (map icons) © drmakkoy/Getty Images.
p18 (oil well) Image on page 18 used under licence from Shutterstock.com.
p20 (Google offices) SpVVK/iStock Editorial / Getty Images Plus. p20 (map icons) © drmakkoy/Getty Images.
p21 (Grand Canyon) Image on page 21 used under licence from Shutterstock.com.

Section Three — Southern North America
p22 (cacti) © drmakkoy/Getty Images. p24 (oil well) Image on pages 24 used under licence from Shutterstock.com.
p24 (man harvesting bananas) © robertharding / Alamy Stock Photo.
p26 (oil well) Image on p26 used under licence from Shutterstock.com.
p26 (waterfall icon) Image on page 26 used under licence from Shutterstock.com.

Section Four — South America
p26 (Catatumbo lightning) © mauritius images GmbH / Alamy Stock Photo. p28 (Rio statue) © drmakkoy/DigitalVision Vectors/via Getty Images. p29 (Yanomami yano) © Robin Tenison / robertharding/Getty Images. p29 (deforestation) © iStock.com/VasjaKoman.
p30 (cacti) © drmakkoy/Getty Images. p30 (dam) © Dmitrii Kholiavskii / Alamy Stock Vector. p32 (oil well) Image on page 32 used under licence from Shutterstock.com.

Inside cover
(old blank paper) © iStock.com/tomograf.